D0336768

Flowchart Science

FORCES

Mary Colson

raintree

a Capstone company — publishers for children

Raintree is an imprint of Capstone Global Library Limited, a company incorporated in England and Wales having its registered office at 264 Banbury Road, Oxford OX2 7DY – Registered company number: 6695582

www.raintree.co.uk
myorders@raintree.co.uk

Text © Capstone Global Library Limited 2017
The moral rights of the proprietor have been asserted.

All rights reserved. No part of this publication may be reproduced in any form or by any means (including photocopying or storing it in any medium by electronic means and whether or not transiently or incidentally to some other use of this publication) without the written permission of the copyright owner, except in accordance with the provisions of the Copyright, Designs and Patents Act 1988 or under the terms of a licence issued by the Copyright Licensing Agency, Saffron House, 6–10 Kirby Street, London EC1N 8TS (www.cla.co.uk). Applications for the copyright owner's written permission should be addressed to the publisher.

Produced for Raintree by Calcium
Edited by Sarah Eason and Amanda Learmonth
Designed by Simon Borrough
Picture research by Susannah Jayes
Production by Victoria Fitzgerald
Originated by Capstone Global Library Ltd © 2016
Printed and bound in China

ISBN 978 1 4747 3130 0
20 19 18 17 16
10 9 8 7 6 5 4 3 2 1

British Library Cataloguing in Publication Data
A full catalogue record for this book is available from the British Library

Acknowledgements
We would like to thank the following for permission to reproduce photographs:
Shutterstock: Andrey Armyagov 24–25, Claudio Bertoloni 1, 21r, Bikeriderlondon 6–7, Andrew Burgess 20–21, Daxiao Productions 6b, Fotos593 12–13, Filip Fuxa 38–39, Hellen Grig 41r, IM Photo 18–19, Irin K 33t, Jabiru 4–5, JLR Photography 28–29, Luciano Mortula 15t, Nagel Photography 13b, Ostill 44–45, Jose Antonio Perez 26–27, Samot 9t, Stefan Schurr 27b, Seqoya 8–9, SpeedKingz 34–35, Stocker1970 40–41, Vicspacewalker 29r, Tom Wang 14–15, Christopher Wood 32–33.

Cover art reproduced with permission of:
Shutterstock: Denkcreative, Lineartestpilot.

Every effort has been made to contact copyright holders of material reproduced in this book. Any omissions will be rectified in subsequent printings if notice is given to the publisher.

All the internet addresses (URLs) given in this book were valid at the time of going to press. However, due to the dynamic nature of the internet, some addresses may have changed, or sites may have changed or ceased to exist since publication. While the author and publisher regret any inconvenience this may cause readers, no responsibility for any such changes can be accepted by either the author or the publisher.

LEWISHAM LIBRARY SERVICE	
Askews & Holts	28-Apr-2017
J531.6 JUNIOR NON-FI	\

Contents

Chapter 1
The power of forces

Forces are some of the most powerful things in the universe, but you cannot see them. They're all around us and you can't even feel them, but you can sometimes feel their effects. A force is a push or a pull. When you push or pull an object, you apply force to the object. Forces can make things speed up, slow down, move forwards or backwards, twist, rise, fall or stay still.

You use forces every day. In the morning, you get up, get dressed and have breakfast. You might switch on a light, open a door, turn on the shower, rub yourself dry with a towel, pour cereal into a bowl and lift a spoon. All these actions require different forces to make them possible. In humans and other animals, muscles produce the force to move body parts. On a much larger scale, planets, stars and moons in the solar system encounter far more powerful forces.

This book explores the forces around us every day. It explains how forces work and how they move an object or hold materials together, and helps you understand how forces are a part of our existence. You will also learn that without forces, life itself would be impossible.

Roller coasters speed downhill and around corners. You can feel the effects of forces on your body as the track twists and turns.

Balanced forces

Once an object is moving, it continues to move until another force makes it speed up, slow down, change direction, change shape or stop. Forces combine to create a bigger force. Imagine two horses harnessed together to pull a cart. They pull the cart more quickly and easily than a single horse because they are combining their forces.

To make something move, one force must be stronger than another. In a tug-of-war, if two teams are pulling in opposite directions with equal force, there is balance. The rope does not move. This balance is called **equilibrium**. **Balanced forces** do not cause a change in motion. They are equal in size and opposite in direction.

Unbalanced forces are not equal in size and direction. When one force is stronger than another we get an unbalanced force. We use these forces to cause objects to move, speed up, slow down, stop or change direction.

The child that is closest in this photograph is heavier than the one that is further away. The forces are unbalanced and the see-saw moves.

Gymnasts use the strength of their muscles to create equilibrium and balance in challenging positions.

Get smart!

The English physicist and mathematician Isaac Newton (1642-1727) is considered to be one of the most important scientists of all time. Among his many achievements, he proposed several laws of motion, which explain how forces work. He said that an object in motion will stay in motion unless it is acted upon by an outside force. He also said every action has an equal and opposite reaction.

Today, force is measured in newtons using a force meter. A force meter has internal springs that measure the size of the stretching force on a scale. Some of these devices can measure forces up to 100 newtons, which is equivalent to a 10.2-kilogramme (22.5-pound) force.

The effects of friction

Friction is a force that prevents two surfaces from moving across each other. When you hit a tennis ball or roll it along the ground, friction opposes the motion, and eventually slows or stops the ball. Friction does not only exist between two solid surfaces. Think about a boat on water – the water rubbing against the bottom of the boat slows it down. When riding a bicycle downhill, there is friction between the wheels and the road surface, which slows you down.

The strength of the force of friction depends on the surfaces rubbing together. If the surfaces are smooth, there will be less friction than if they are rough. You slide on ice because the ice is very smooth and there is little friction. Friction can also generate heat. On a cold day, you rub your hands together to keep warm. It is the force of friction between the surfaces of your hands that makes them warm up.

A camel's feet are flat and wide. The large area increases the friction between the foot and the sand. This helps the camel to grip the sand better and stop it from sinking down into the sand.

The soles of your shoes grip the ground as you walk. Friction causes this grip, whether you are walking on a pavement, sand, grass or gravel. On a very smooth surface, such as ice, there is less friction and the soles of your shoes may not have enough grip to stop you from falling over.

Tractors have huge tyres with lots of **tread**. This increases friction on muddy ground, and stops them from getting stuck. In contrast, professional cyclists use very thin, smooth tyres called slicks to minimize friction and grip, and help them move as fast as possible.

Skiers wax the bottom of their skis to reduce the friction between the skis and the snow, which allows them to travel faster.

Get flowchart smart!

Balanced and unbalanced forces

Follow this flowchart to take a look at how balanced and unbalanced forces work in a see-saw.

An empty see-saw is a level plank balanced on both sides of a pivot. The forces acting on both ends of the see-saw are equal.

When somebody sits on one end of the see-saw, the forces become unbalanced.

If the second person is heavier than the first person, the see-saw will be unbalanced again. The lighter person will be on the higher end of the see-saw.

The unbalanced forces cause a change in motion, and one end of the see-saw moves down.

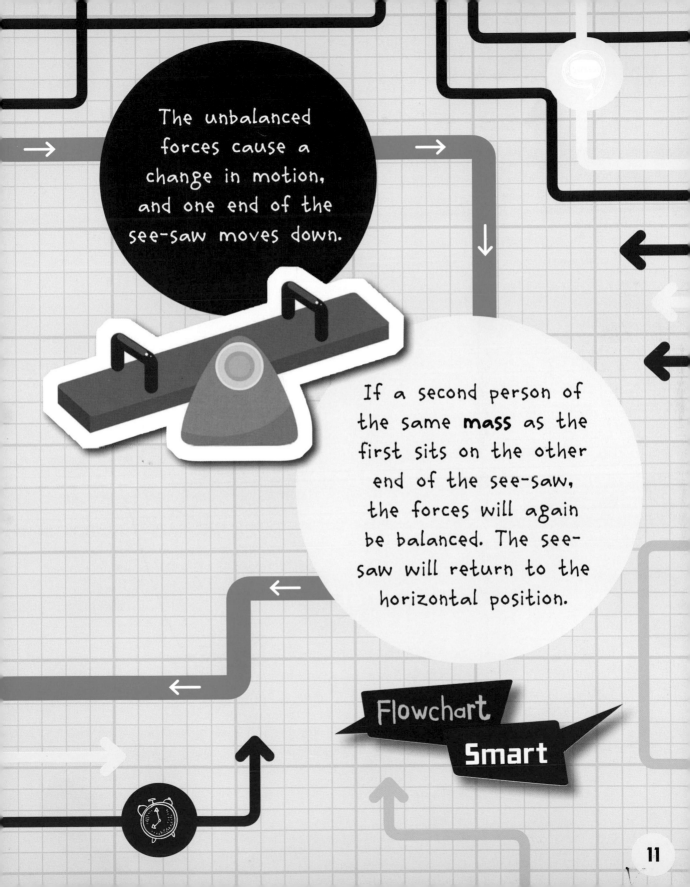

If a second person of the same **mass** as the first sits on the other end of the see-saw, the forces will again be balanced. The see-saw will return to the horizontal position.

Flowchart
Smart

11

Chapter 2

Forces that shape Earth

Every day, all over the world, forces change planet Earth. High above the surface, deep under water and far underground, forces are at work. The downward force of the atmosphere and the movement of ocean currents cause Earth to wobble and shift by approximately 7 metres (23 feet) every 400 days as it spins on its axis. We don't notice this wobble, but we do notice other forces that impact the landscape and the weather, too.

Some of the most powerful natural forces that shape Earth's surface are volcanoes. A volcano is a hole in Earth's crust, which is the rocky outer shell of the planet. Often, a volcano is a tall mountain, but it can also be a large, low mound. Inside a volcano is a chamber of molten rock called **magma**. When the pressure inside the magma chamber becomes too great, it pushes up through the **volcanic vent**. Once the magma erupts through Earth's surface, it's called lava. A river of red-hot lava can quickly burn anything in its path.

Get smart!

Volcanoes come in all different shapes and sizes. The force of a volcanic eruption can also vary. Scientists called volcanologists measure the strength of a volcanic eruption using the Volcanic Explosivity Index (VEI). This scale runs from 0 to 8. A level 8 eruption is "mega-colossal", producing thousands of cubic kilometres of lava, an ash cloud more than 25 kilometres (15 miles) high and causing widespread devastation to the environment. Huge quantities of ash released into the atmosphere would block the sunlight, altering Earth's climate for many years.

It's very difficult to predict exactly when an eruption will occur. Some volcanoes erupt continuously, while others erupt only every few thousand years.

The water in this hot spring in the volcanic area of Yellowstone National Park in the United States has been heated by hot molten rock beneath Earth's surface.

Tectonic forces

Earth's surface is made up of massive sections of rock called **tectonic plates**. The plates move constantly and push slowly past, towards or away from each other. As the plates move, forces are exerted on themselves and each other. Sometimes, the pressure between two plates builds up and is suddenly released as the plates move past one another. This creates powerful waves of **energy** that we feel as an earthquake. Every year, more than 1 million earthquakes shake Earth's surface.

Earth's plates move at different speeds and in different directions. When plates pull apart from each other, magma rises up from below Earth's surface and forms new crust. When plates push towards each other, the edges of the plates are forced upwards and can form mountain ranges. When the plates try to slide past each other horizontally, they often lock and then suddenly release, causing an earthquake. The San Andreas Fault in California, United States, is the boundary between the North American and Pacific plates, which move in this way.

Earthquakes can quickly and dramatically scar natural landscapes and man-made structures, such as this motorway.

In San Francisco, United States, there is a high risk of earthquakes. Many tall buildings are earthquake-proof. They have wide bases and are designed to bend and flex like a wave.

Get smart!

It's not easy to predict earthquakes, and very often they occur without warning. Scientists called seismologists study earthquakes. They use devices called seismometers to help them predict the timing and measure the strength of an earthquake. Seismometers pick up vibrations in Earth's crust. An increase in vibrations might indicate an impending earthquake. Earthquakes are measured on the Moment Magnitude Scale. A magnitude "8" earthquake can totally destroy communities near the epicentre.

Get flowchart smart!

What forces cause volcanoes to erupt?

Follow the flowchart to examine what happens during a volcanic eruption.

Deep inside a volcano is a vast magma chamber. This is a reservoir of red-hot molten rock.

Gases and rocks ripped loose from inside the volcano are also thrown up into the atmosphere.

The lava and rocks fall back to Earth as dust, ash and **pumice**.

When the magma rises in the chamber, the pressure inside it increases.

The pressure forces magma up through weak points called vents in the volcano's solid rock.

When the magma reaches the surface, it erupts out of the volcano. It is now called lava.

Flowchart Smart

Chapter 3
Forces in air and water

Air has **weight** and exerts pressure on everything it touches. On the surface of Earth we are essentially at the bottom of a large pool of air. We call this air the atmosphere. It is the weight of the atmosphere pushing down on Earth that gives us atmospheric pressure. Atmospheric pressure is often measured using a barometer. The closer to the surface of the planet, the greater the atmospheric pressure. As you move upwards, away from Earth's surface, the atmospheric pressure drops because there is less air pushing down.

Aeroplane cabins are carefully pressurized so that humans can travel safely without suffering the effects of low atmospheric pressure.

At sea level, the atmosphere presses down on your body at around 1 atmosphere (atm) – this is a unit of atmospheric pressure equivalent to 1 kilogramme per square centimetre (14.5 pounds per square inch). You don't feel this force because the fluid in your body pushes back with the same force and creates balance. A change in atmospheric pressure is important for forecasters because it indicates a change in the weather. A low-pressure system often brings rainy weather, and a high-pressure system usually brings clear weather.

Water also has weight and can exert a force. In a swimming pool, water presses on all parts of your body. The deeper you move below the surface of the water, the greater the pressure change. If you dive down to the deep end of a swimming pool, you might feel this pressure in your ears. For every 10 m (33 ft.) you go beneath the surface of the water, the pressure increases by 1 atm. The human body can't cope with the high pressure deep beneath the oceans. The water pressure causes any space that's filled with air, such as the lungs, to collapse.

Get smart!

Pressure is a force applied over a specific area. If a force is applied to a small area, the pressure is great; if the same force is applied to a larger area, the pressure is lower. Blaise Pascal (1623-1662) was a French mathematician. Among his many achievements, he experimented with atmospheric pressure and how it can be estimated in terms of weight. Pressure can be measured in pascals in honour of his groundbreaking work.

Forces: up, down and sideways

Forces can push or pull in any direction. When something pushes down on water, the water pushes back up. The force of water pushing back is called upthrust. When you're in the sea or a pool, press a ball down into the water. The resisting force that you can feel is upthrust. An object in water weighs less than it does in the air. This is because the upthrust of the water cancels out some of the gravitational force pulling the object down. The size of the upthrust force in water depends on the amount of water **displaced** (pushed out of the way). When upthrust is equal to or greater than the object's weight, the object will float. If the upthrust is less than the object's weight, the object will sink.

Penguins have pointed beaks, smooth feathers and a streamlined shape. They experience little drag and can swim very fast.

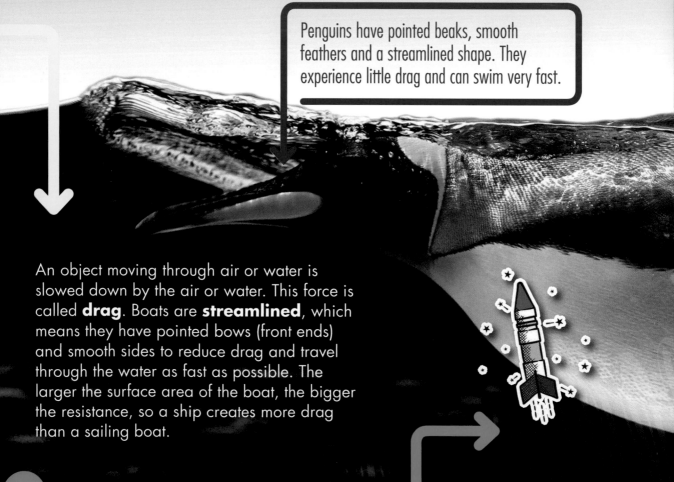

An object moving through air or water is slowed down by the air or water. This force is called **drag**. Boats are **streamlined**, which means they have pointed bows (front ends) and smooth sides to reduce drag and travel through the water as fast as possible. The larger the surface area of the boat, the bigger the resistance, so a ship creates more drag than a sailing boat.

Aerodynamics is the science that studies the interaction between air and the solid bodies moving through it. Think about some of the man-made and natural shapes that travel through air. Rockets, planes, arrows and bullets are all streamlined, or aerodynamic. They have a smooth, slim shape that offers the least resistance to the air, and can therefore travel at high speeds. In the natural world, birds have aerodynamic shapes to help them fly.

Racing cyclists wear tight clothing to create a more streamlined shape, reduce drag and travel faster.

Get flowchart smart!

How to use water forces

Use this flowchart to look at the forces at work when a person goes waterskiing.

The waterskier rests in the water with the tips of the skis above the water's surface. The waterskier holds on to a handle at the end of a rope attached to a speedboat.

The waterskier leans backwards slightly to balance the pull of the boat.

As the boat begins to pull the waterskier, the angled skis apply pressure to the water to counter the pull of the boat.

The water is pushed downwards by the bottoms of the skis.

The acceleration of the boat and the upward angle of the skis creates an upward force that lifts the waterskier out of the water and into a standing position.

Flowchart Smart

Chapter 4

Gravity: the universal force

Gravity affects everything on Earth. It is the force that holds people and all objects on the surface of the planet. If you throw a ball up into the air, the force of gravity slows it down and causes it to fall. The atmosphere and oceans are kept in place by the force of gravity. Without it, the atmosphere would drift off into space and life on Earth would be impossible.

All objects exert gravity on their surroundings, and the strength of their gravity depends on their mass. The Moon has a smaller mass than Earth, which is why its force of gravity is less. The astronauts who landed on the Moon wore heavy spacesuits. These suits felt much heavier on Earth than on the Moon. Jupiter is the largest planet in the solar system. Its pull of gravity is stronger than Earth's. It would take more force to walk, run or jump on Jupiter. The world record for the long jump on Earth is more than 8 m (26 ft.) On Jupiter, it would be around only 3 m (10 ft.)

On a spacewalk, an astronaut experiences no gravitational force. As a result, the spacesuit feels far less cumbersome than it does on Earth.

Get smart!

An object's weight and its mass are two different things. The mass of an object is the amount of **matter** in the object. You have a mass that is made up of your bones, muscles, fluids and other body parts. Your mass does not change, no matter where you are, because there's still the same amount of you. However, your weight changes depending on your location. Weight is a measure of how strongly gravity pulls on an object. If you weigh yourself at the equator, you will weigh slightly less than at the North Pole, where there is a stronger **gravitational pull.**

Forces in space

In space, the stars, moons and planets keep their positions and orbits as a result of gravity. In the 17th century, Isaac Newton realized that gravity on Earth is the same force that keeps the Moon orbiting Earth, and all the planets moving around the Sun. But how does this force work?

Every object in the universe that has mass exerts a gravitational pull on every other mass. Humans have some gravitational pull because we have mass, but we are tiny in comparison to Earth or Mars, which have enormous masses. Earth has enough gravitational pull to hold the atmosphere in place around the planet, but smaller objects in space, such as Pluto, may not have enough gravitational pull to hold an atmosphere. The Sun is 1.37 million km (850,000 mi.) wide – more than 100 times wider than Earth. It has a huge mass and a very strong gravitational pull. The Sun's pull is so powerful that it holds all the planets in our solar system in their orbits around it.

The gravitational pull of a planet also varies depending on the planet's density. Neptune has 17 times Earth's mass, but it is also far larger, meaning it has a low density. As a result, its gravitational pull is only slightly greater than Earth's.

A spaceship needs a lot of force to help it reach the speed required to break free from Earth's gravitational pull. The orange fuel tank will be released once it has helped the rocket into space.

Get smart!

Spaceships need a lot of power to escape Earth's gravitational force. The speed at which they must travel to leave Earth's atmosphere is called the **escape velocity**. A rocket accelerates to 40,200 km [25,000 mi.] per hour to get into orbit above Earth's atmosphere. The further away from the centre of Earth an object is, the lower the pull of gravity.

A high jumper must generate enough upward force in order to briefly counteract Earth's gravity and jump over the pole.

Tides and waves

The gravitational forces of the Sun and Moon, combined with the **rotation** of Earth, cause tides in Earth's seas and oceans. These large bodies of water are constantly rising and falling depending on the position of the Moon and Sun. As the Moon passes overhead, the force of its gravity lifts the ocean water to form a bulge or a "high tide". Once the Moon has passed, the water level falls back to its "low tide" position. This powerful force affects land too, but because Earth is solid, the land does not move as dramatically. A spring tide takes place when the Moon, Sun and Earth are in a line. The gravity of the Moon and Sun combines and pulls in the same direction to create an unusually high and low tide on Earth.

As a wave approaches the shore, the bottom of the wave slows down as it meets solid ground. The top part of the wave continues to move forwards and eventually tips over as the wave breaks.

Surfers, sailors and bodyboarders use the force of the waves for their leisure activities. But what is a wave and how do its forces work? A wave is a moving disturbance that travels through space and matter. As it moves, it transfers energy from one place to another. If you throw a stone into a pond, you can see waves in the form of ripples. If you go to the beach, you can see large waves roll in and move back out.

In water, waves are called **transverse waves**. This is because the disturbance moves at right angles to the direction of the wave. In the oceans, water moves up and down as the wave passes horizontally. Ocean waves are generated by wind moving across the water's surface. Occasionally, a powerful earthquake on the ocean floor generates a massive tsunami.

The Dead Sea is extremely salty. This makes its water very dense and gives it more upward force than normal seawater. It is a smaller body of water than an ocean, and has smaller waves.

Get flowchart smart!

29

Launching rockets

Use this flowchart to find out how rockets overcome Earth's gravity.

A rocket's engines are started and hot gases fire downwards towards Earth, creating an enormous force.

This produces an equal yet opposite force that pushes the rocket upwards. This is called thrust.

Once the rocket is 100 kilometres (62 miles) from Earth, it has entered space.

The rocket must travel at approximately 11 km (7 mi.) per second to escape Earth's gravity. This is the escape velocity and is equivalent to a speed of 40,200 km (25,000 mi.) per hour.

Most of the rocket's fuel is used to achieve the required escape velocity.

When a tank of fuel is used up, it is released from the rocket. This makes the rocket lighter and means it needs less force to travel onwards.

Flowchart
Smart

Chapter 5
Magnetic force

A magnet is a piece of metal that attracts another metal. The force it uses to do this is called magnetism. You can't see this force, but you can see its effects. The area around a magnet is called a **magnetic field**. If you place an object in a magnetic field, it will be affected by the magnet. Test it out for yourself. Pick up a fridge magnet and slowly move it towards a fridge. As you approach the fridge, you will feel the magnetic attraction of the magnet. This means the fridge is within the magnetic field of the magnet. The pull will be strongest when the magnet is very close to the fridge.

Earth's magnetic north and south poles are located very close to its geographic North and South Poles. Compass needles line up in a north-south orientation between the two poles.

Get smart!

Deep in space, some objects have a magnetic force many billions of times greater than any on Earth, or elsewhere in the solar system. Scientists use special telescopes to learn about mysterious "magnetars". These phenomena were once gigantic stars, but they have since collapsed and exploded in a supernova. What remains is the core of a star, which is very dense and highly magnetic.

Bees, dolphins, lobsters and pigeons have tiny magnets in their bodies that enable them to navigate.

Nickel and iron are metals that are magnetic. At the very centre of Earth is an inner core of liquid iron. This makes Earth behave like a giant magnet. All magnets, including Earth, have two poles – north and south. Opposites attract, which means that the north pole of one magnet is attracted to the south pole of another. If two north poles or two south poles come together, there is no magnetic pull between them. Instead, they will push apart, or repel.

Earth's magnetic field protects the planet from radiation and damaging particles from the Sun. The magnetic field acts like a shield that deflects these harmful particles back out into space.

Using magnetic forces

You might be surprised by how many uses there are for magnets in everyday life. For example, bags, mobile phone cases and kitchen cabinets often close using magnets. Magnetic paper clip holders can help keep desks tidy. Fridge magnets hold pictures, shopping lists and other items. Household recycling is even sorted using magnets. Recycling centres separate magnetic materials, such as steel cans, from other waste. Magnets are found inside televisions, computers, doorbells and music entertainment systems.

Superfast maglev trains use magnetism to travel at incredible speeds of up to 550 km (340 mi.) per hour. Maglev means "magnetic levitation" or "lifted up by magnets". Magnetic repulsion between **electromagnets** in the track and the underside of the train lift the train, which appears to float above the track. There is no friction between the train and the rails, so it can travel very fast.

Doctors use magnets to look inside patients' bodies. The patient lies inside a magnetic ring in a Magnetic Resonance Imaging (MRI) scanner. The magnet is very powerful so any metallic objects, such as keys or watches, must be removed before the magnet is turned on. MRI scans create detailed images of a person's internal organs, so doctors can see whether there is any damage or disease. MRI scanners can study the brain to detect which parts are used for different activities, highlight any areas of damage and detect changes as the patient experiences different emotions.

An MRI scan of a human head is used to check the blood flow to the brain and look for any blood clots, vessel problems or tumours.

Get flowchart smart!

How magnets work

Follow the flowchart to examine magnets and their magnetic fields.

Magnets are objects that produce an area of magnetic force called a magnetic field.

Magnetic poles behave differently. Opposite poles attract (pull towards each other) while like poles repel (push away).

Magnets are usually made from iron or another metal that contains lots of iron, such as steel.

A magnet attracts other objects that are made of iron, or contain iron. This invisible force is called magnetism.

A magnet has two poles: the north pole and the south pole. The magnet is strongest or has the most force at its poles.

Flowchart Smart

Chapter 6

Making forces work

For thousands of years, humans have known the importance of forces. The mighty monuments of the ancient world, such as the Acropolis in Greece and the pyramids in Egypt, could only have been built using an understanding of forces. Simple machines, such as levers, have always been extremely useful. A lever is a solid bar that rests on a pivot and is used to lift **loads**. The user exerts a small amount of force on one end of the lever in order to generate a much greater force at the other end.

A pulley is another simple machine. It consists of one or more wheels and a rope. A load is attached to one end of a rope, which is then passed around the edge of a wheel. A groove in the wheel keeps the rope in place. Pulleys change the direction of a force. If you pull down on the rope, it lifts the load. Clothes lines and flagpoles use pulleys. Movable pulleys provide us with a **mechanical advantage**. They allow us to lift objects that would normally be too heavy. In the construction industry, tower cranes are used to raise very heavy loads. These enormous cranes use balanced and unbalanced forces to keep them upright. They also use pulleys, wheels and gears in their motors to winch objects high into the air.

Get smart!

The stone blocks used to build the Egyptian pyramids 4,500 years ago weigh many tonnes. They are far too heavy to have been carried to the top of the structures. Many historians believe that pulleys and ramps were used to lift the stones, but no one knows for sure. No one has ever discovered any evidence of the infrastructure used to build the pyramids.

Stonehenge was built 4,000 years ago. The stones came from a quarry 400 km (250 mi.) away. They may have been dragged on rollers and then transported by water.

Forces and shapes

Imagine a piece of clay. Think about rolling it, twisting it, pushing it and pulling it into a different shape. You might make a vase, a bowl or a figure of a person. You exert a force on the clay to make it change shape. Some shapes are stronger than others and require greater force in order to be bent or changed. Scientists, designers, architects and engineers use the knowledge of a material's strength to create lasting objects, from small items of furniture to towering skyscrapers.

Get smart!

Next time you look at a building or a bridge, notice the use of circles and triangles. These two shapes are very strong and can bear the heaviest loads. Suspension bridges, such as the Humber Bridge in East Yorkshire, use triangles. Thousands of years ago, the ancient Romans and Greeks knew about the strength of circles and triangles, and these shapes are visible in many ancient buildings. The next strongest shape is an arch, which was used to build many old cathedrals and bridges.

All solid structures and objects have a shape. The shape must be strong enough to serve the object's purpose. For example, in the natural world, a feather's shape helps birds to fly and keeps them warm. Spiders' webs are shaped to help a spider catch its prey. At home or at school, a piece of paper needs enough strength to be written on. A pen must not collapse when it is held. Larger objects, such as cars, bridges, fairground rides and aeroplanes, need the best shape to support and protect their loads.

The Clifton Suspension Bridge in Bristol uses strong shapes like triangles and arches to support the suspension cables and the deck.

Spiders' webs are shaped to withstand huge forces. If a strand of the web is broken, the overall strength of the web increases rather than decreases.

Get flowchart smart!

41

How cranes use forces

Following this flowchart, let's take a look at how cranes are constructed and how they raise loads using forces.

The base of a crane is fixed securely to concrete on the ground. The tower is built using many triangle shapes for strength.

Inside the cabin, limit switches tell the crane driver if the crane is becoming overloaded. Without these, the forces could become unbalanced and the crane could drop the load or collapse.

The load is suspended from a horizontal **jib** (arm). A trolley runs along the jib to move the load.

A motor and gears are located in the machinery arm. The **counterweights**, which help balance the crane, are also here.

If the load is lifted near the centre of the crane, the crane can lift more weight. If the load is lifted at the furthest end of the jib, away from the centre, the crane can only lift a lighter load.

The motor lifts the load using the gears.

Flowchart Smart

Feel the force

We may not be able to see forces, but we can certainly feel their effects. Forces shape our very existence. We couldn't move, talk, eat, sleep or even breathe without forces. There would be no atmosphere around the planet and life on Earth would simply not be possible.

For millennia, people have used forces to create amazing structures that we still marvel at today. Scientists and engineers use their knowledge of forces to explore space, develop new technologies and generate clean energy. Space rockets and satellites use forces to escape the gravitational pull of Earth to go into and explore space. Super-strength magnets are being developed that could power the cars of the future, instead of petrol. Wind turbines and **hydroelectric power** plants harness natural forces to generate electricity.

From the small-scale forces that enable our daily lives, to the powerful, Earth-shaping forces of plate tectonics, earthquakes and volcanic eruptions, forces are all around us. With our increased knowledge and understanding of forces and how they work, an exciting future full of possibilities awaits.

Understanding forces better can mean the difference between winning and losing. Sports scientists have an extensive knowledge of how muscles use forces and react to training. This means that precise training programmes can be made for individual athletes to help them run faster or for longer, or jump further or higher. Better understanding of aerodynamics is helping cyclists travel more quickly as bikes are redesigned and rider positions adjusted.

Many American football players now wear helmets containing single-pole magnets. It's hoped that repelling forces in the helmets will reduce head injuries.

Glossary

aerodynamics science of the way in which objects move through air

balanced forces two forces that are equal and act in opposite directions on an object

counterweight weight that provides a balance against something of equal weight

displaced moved physically out of position

drag resistant force exerted by air or water on an object

electromagnet object that becomes magnetic when an electric current is passed near or through it

energy ability of an object or material do to work, such as to cause movement

equilibrium state of equal balance between opposing forces

escape velocity speed an object needs to reach to escape Earth's gravitational pull

force push or pull

gravitational pull force of attraction between all objects, large or small

hydroelectric power energy harnessed from moving water

jib horizontal loading arm of a tower crane

load total weight that a structure is designed to carry or support

magma hot molten rock beneath Earth's crust

magnetic field space near a magnetic object in which magnetic forces can be detected

mass quantity of matter that an object or material contains

matter substance that makes up everything in the universe

mechanical advantage use of pulleys and ropes to enable the moving of an object using less force

pumice lightweight volcanic rock formed when frothy lava solidifies

rotation motion of an object around an internal axis

streamlined designed to move easily and quickly through air or water

strength strong or powerful quality or state of being

tectonic plate enormous piece of Earth's crust that moves around on magma

transverse wave wave in which the forces that create the wave move at right angles to the direction of the wave

tread pattern of raised lines and grooves on the surface of a tyre that help improve grip

unbalanced forces two forces that are not equal and act in opposite directions on an object

volcanic vent weak area in Earth's crust from which magma can escape

weight force of gravitational attraction between two objects

Find out more

Books

Forces and Magnets (Moving Up with Science), Peter Riley (Franklin Watts, 2016)

Forces and Motion (Mind Webs), Anna Claybourne (Wayland, 2016)

Ride that Rollercoaster! Forces at an Amusement Park (Feel the Force), Louise Spilsbury and Richard Spilsbury (Raintree, 2016)

Websites

Watch this fun video about the scientist Isaac Newton:
www.bbc.co.uk/education/clips/zcc9wmn

Take a quiz challenge all about forces and motion:
www.dkfindout.com/uk/science/forces-and-motion

Check out more facts about magnets and magnetic fields at:
nationalgeographic.org/encyclopedia/magnetism

Discover more about volcanoes here:
www.ngkids.co.uk/science-and-nature/Volcano-Facts

Index